Book 1
C Programming Professional
Made Easy

BY SAM KEY

&

Book 2
Rails Programming
Professional Made Easy

BY SAM KEY

Book 1
C Programming Professional Made Easy

BY SAM KEY

Expert C Programming Language Success In A Day For Any Computer User!

Programming Box Set #25: C Programming Professional Made Easy & Rails Programming Professional Made Easy

Table Of Contents

Introduction.. 5

Chapter 1 The Basic Elements Of C 6

Chapter 2 What is C Programming Language...................................... 17

Chapter 3 Understanding C Program...19

Chapter 4 Learn C Programming.. 21

Conclusion 32

Introduction

I want to thank you and congratulate you for purchasing the book, "Professional C Programming Made Easy: Expert C Programming Language Success In A Day For Any Computer User!".

This book contains proven steps and strategies on how to understand and perform C programming. C is one of the most basic programming tools used for a wide array of applications. Most people stay away from it because the language seem complicated, with all those characters, letters, sequences and special symbols.

This book will break down every element and explain in detail each language used in the C program. By the time you are done with this book, C programming language will be easy to understand and easy to execute.

Read on and learn.

Thanks again for purchasing this book. I hope you enjoy it!

Chapter 1 The Basic Elements Of C

The seemingly complicated C program is composed of the following basic elements:

Character Set

The alphabet in both upper and lower cases is used in C. The 0-9 digits are also used, including white spaces and some special characters. These are used in different combinations to form elements of a basic C program such as expressions, constants, variables, etc.

Special characters include the following:

+ ,. *− / % = & ! #?"^ '| / ( )< > { } [ ] ;: @ ~!

White spaces include:

- Blank space

- Carriage return

- Horizontal tab

- Form feed

- New line

Identifiers

An identifier is a name given to the various elements of the C program, such as arrays, variables and functions. These contain digits and letters in various arrangements. However, identifiers should always start with a letter. The letters may be in upper case, lower case or both. However, these are not interchangeable. C programming is case sensitive, as each letter in different cases is regarded as separate from each other. Underscores are also permitted because it is considered by the program as a kind of letter.

Examples of valid identifiers include the following:

ab123

A

stud_name

average

velocity

TOTAL

Identifiers need to start with a letter and should not contain illegal characters. Examples of invalid identifiers include the following:

2nd — should always start with a letter

"Jamshedpur" — contains the illegal character (")

stud name — contains a blank space, which is an illegal character

stud-name — contains an illegal character (-)

In C, a single identifier may be used to refer to a number of different entities within the same C program. For instance, an array and a variable can share one identifier. For example:

The variable is int difference, average, A[5]; // sum, average

The identifier is A[5].

In the same program, an array can be named A, too.

__func__

The __func__ is a predefined identifier that provides functions names and makes these accessible and ready for use anytime in the function. The complier would automatically declare the __func__ immediately after placing the opening brace when declaring the function definitions. The compiler declares the predefined identifier this way:

static const char __func__[] = "Alex";

"Alex" refers to a specific name of this particular function.

Take a look at this example:

```
#include <stdio.h>


void anna1(void)   {

    printf("%sn",__func__);

    return;

}


int main() {

    myfunc();

}
```

What will appear as an output will be anna1

Keywords

Reserved words in C that come with standard and predefined meanings are called keywords. The uses for these words are restricted to their predefined intended purpose. Keywords cannot be utilized as programmer-defined identifiers. In C, there are 32 keywords being used, which include the following:

auto	default
break	double
char	float
case	else
continue	extern
const	enum
do	goto

for	switch
if	typedef
long	struct
int	union
register	switch
short	void
return	unsigned
sizeof	while
signed	volatile

Data Types

There are different types of data values that are passed in C. Each of the types of data has different representations within the memory bank of the computer. These also have varying memory requirements. Data type modifiers/qualifiers are often used to augment the different types of data.

Supported data types in C include int, char, float, double, void, _Bool, _Complex, arrays, and constants.

int

Integer quantities are stored in this type of data. The data type *int* can store a collection of different values, starting from INT_MAX to INT_MIN. An in-header file, <limits h>, defines the range.

These int data types use type modifiers such as unsigned, signed, long, long long and short.

Short int means that they occupy memory space of only 2 bytes.

A long int uses 4 bytes of memory space.

Short unsigned int is a data type that uses 2 bytes of memory space and store positive values only, ranging from 0 to 65535.

Unsigned int requires memory space similar to that of short unsigned int. For regular and ordinary int, the bit at the leftmost portion is used for the integer's sign.

Long unsigned int uses 4 bytes of space. It stores all positive integers ranging from 0 to 4294967295.

An int data is automatically considered as signed.

Long long int data type uses 64 bits memory. This type may either be unsigned or signed. Signed long long data type can store values ranging from −9,223,372,036,854,775,808 to 9,223,372,036,854,775,807. Unsigned long long data type stores value range of 0 to 18,446,744,073,709,551,615.

char

Single characters such as those found in C program's character set are stored by this type of data. The char data type uses 1 byte in the computer's memory. Any value from C program's character set can be stored as char. Modifiers that can be used are either unsigned or signed.

A char would always use 1 byte in the computer's memory space, whether it is signed or unsigned. The difference is on the value range. Values that can be stored as unsigned char range from 0 to 255. Signed char stores values ranging from −128 to +127. By default, a char data type is considered unsigned.

For each of the char types, there is a corresponding integer interpretation. This makes each char a special short integer.

float

A float is a data type used in storing real numbers that have single precision. That is, precision denoted as having 6 more digits after a decimal point. Float data type uses 4 bytes memory space.

The modifier for this data type is long, which uses the same memory space as that of double data type.

double

The double data type is used for storing real numbers that have double precision. Memory space used is 8 bytes. Double data type uses long as a type modifier. This uses up memory storage space of 10 bytes.

void

Void data type is used for specifying empty sets, which do not contain any value. Hence, void data type also occupies no space (0 bytes) in the memory storage.

_Bool

This is a Boolean type of data. It is an unsigned type of integer. It stores only 2 values, which is 0 and 1. When using _Bool, include **<stdboolh>**.

_Complex

This is used for storing complex numbers. In C, three types of _Complex are used. There is the float _Complex, double _Complex, and long double _Complex. These are found in <complex h> file.

Arrays

This identifier is used in referring to the collection of data that share the same name and of the same type of data. For example, all integers or all characters that have the same name. Each of the data is represented by its own array element. The subscripts differentiate the arrays from each other.

Constants

Constants are identifiers used in C. The values of identifiers do not change anywhere within the program. Constants are declared this way:

const datatype varname = value

const is the keyword that denotes or declares the variable as the fixed value entity, i.e., the constant.

In C, there are 4 basic constants used. These include the integer constant, floating-point, character and string constants. Floating-point and integer types of constant do not contain any blank spaces or commas. Minus signs can be used, which denotes negative quantities.

Integer Constants

11

Integer constants are integer valued numbers consisting of sequence of digits. These can be written using 3 different number systems, namely, decimal, octal and hexadecimal.

Decimal system (base 10)

An integer constant written in the decimal system contains combinations of numbers ranging from 0 to 9. Decimal constants should start with any number other except 0. For example, a decimal constant is written in C as:

const int size =76

Octal (base 8)

Octal constants are any number combinations from 0 to 7. To identify octal constants, the first number should be 0. For example:

const int a= 043; const int b=0;

An octal constant is denoted in the binary form. Take the octal 0347. Each digit is represented as:

$0347 = 011\ 100\ 111 = 3 * 8^2 + 4 * 8^1 + 7 * 8^0 = 231$

3   4   7

Hexadecimal constant (base 16)

This type consists of any of the possible combinations of digits ranging from 0 to 9. This type also includes letters a to f, written in either lowercase or uppercase. To identify hexadecimal constants, these should start with 0X or 0X. For example:

const int c= 0x7FF;

For example, the hexadecimal number 0x2A5 is internally represented in bit patterns within C as:

$0x2A5 = 0010\ 1010\ 0101 = 2 * 16^2 + 10 * 16^1 + 5 * 16^0 = 677$

2   A   5

Wherein, 677 is the decimal equivalent of the hexadecimal number 0x2.

Prefixes for integer constants can either be long or unsigned. A long integer constant (long int) ends with a l of L, such as 67354L or 67354l. The last portion of an unsigned long integer constant should either be ul or UL, such as 672893UL or 672893ul. For an unsigned long long integer constant, UL or ul should be at the last portion. An unsigned constant should end with U or u, such as 673400095u or 673400095U. Normal integer constants are written without any suffix, such as a simple 67458.

Floating Point Constant

This type of constant has a base 10 or base 16 and contains an exponent, a decimal point or both. For a floating point constant with a base 10 and a decimal point, the base is replaced by an E or e. For example, the constant $1.8 * 10^{-3}$ is written as 1.8e-3 or 1.8E-3.

For hexadecimal character constants and the exponent is in the binary form, the exponent is replaced by P or p. Take a look at this example:

This type of constant is often precision quantities. These occupy around 8 bytes of memory. Different add-ons are allowed in some C program versions, such as F for a single precision floating constant or L for a long floating point type of constant.

Character Constant

A sequence of characters, whether single or multiple ones, enclosed by apostrophes or single quotation marks is called a character constant. The character set in the computer determines the integer value equivalent to each character constant. Escape sequences may also be found within the sequence of a character constant.

Single character constants enclosed by apostrophes is internally considered as integers. For example, 'A' is a single character constant that has an integer value of 65. The corresponding integer value is also called the ASCII value. Because of the corresponding numerical value, single character constants can be used in calculations just like how integers are used. Also, these constants can also be used when comparing other types of character constants.

Prefixes used in character constants such as L, U or u are used for character literals. These are considered as wide types of character constants. Character literals with the prefix L are considered under the type wchar_t, which are defined as <stddef.h> under the header file. Character constants that use the prefix U or u are considered as type char16_t or char32_t. These are considered as unsigned types of characters and are defined under the header file as <uchar.h>.

Those that do not have the prefix L are considered a narrow or ordinary character constant. Those that have escape sequences or are composed of at least 2 characters are considered as multicharacter constants.

Escape sequences are a type of character constant used in expressing non-printing characters like carriage return or tab. This sequence always begins with a backward slash, followed by special characters. These sequences represent a single character in the C language even if they are composed of more than 1 character. Examples of some of the most common escape sequences, and their integer (ASCII) value, used in C include the following:

Character	Escape Sequence	ASCII Value
Backspace	\b	008
Bell	\a	007
Newline	\n	010
Null	\o	000
Carriage	\r	013
Horizontal tab	\t	009
Vertical tab	\v	011
Form feed	\f	012

String Literals

Multibyte characters that form a sequence are called string literals. Multibyte characters have bit representations that fit into 1 or more bytes. String literals are enclosed within double quotation marks, for example, "A" and "Anna". There are 2 types of string literals, namely, UTF-8 string literals and wide string literals. Prefixes used for wide string literals include u, U or L. Prefix for UTF-8 string literals is u8.

Additional characters or extended character sets included in string literals are recognized and supported by the compiler. These additional characters can be used meaningfully to further enhance character constants and string literals.

Symbolic constants

Symbolic constants are substitute names for numeric, string or character constants within a program. The compiler would replace the symbolic constants with its actual value once the program is run.

At the beginning of the program, the symbolic constant is defined with a **#define** feature. This feature is called the preprocessor directive.

The definition of a symbolic constant does not end with a semi colon, like other C statements. Take a look at this example:

    #define PI 3.1415

    (//PI is the constant that will represent value 3.1415)

    #define True 1

    #define name "Alice"

For all numeric constants such as floating point and integer, non-numeric characters and blank spaces are not included. These constants are also limited by minimum and maximum bounds, which are usually dependent on the computer.

Variables

Memory locations where data is stored are called variables. These are indicated by a unique identifier. Names for variables are symbolic representations that refer to a particular memory location. Examples are *count, car_no* and *sum*.

Rules when writing the variable names

Writing variable names follow certain rules in order to make sure that data is stored properly and retrieved efficiently.

- Letters (in both lowercase and uppercase), underscore ('_') and digits are the only characters that can be used for variable names.

- Variables should begin either with an underscore or a letter. Starting with an underscore is acceptable, but is not highly recommended. Underscores at the beginning of variables can come in conflict with system names and the compiler may protest.

- There is no limit on the length of variables. The compiler can distinguish the first 31 characters of a variable. This means that individual variables should have different sequences for the 1st 31 characters.

Variables should also be declared at the beginning of a program before it can be used.

Chapter 2 What is C Programming Language?

In C, the programming language is a language that focuses on the structure. It was developed in 1972, at Bell Laboratories, by Dennis Ritchie. The features of the language were derived from "B", which is an earlier programming language and formally known as BCPL or Basic Combined Programming Language. The C programming language was originally developed to implement the UNIX operating system.

Standards of C Programming Language

In 1989, the American National Standards Institute developed the 1st standard specifications. This pioneering standard specification was referred to as C89 and C90, both referring to the same programming language.

In 1999, a revision was made in the programming language. The revised standard was called C99. It had new features such as advanced data types. It also had a few changes, which gave rise to more applications.

The C11 standard was developed, which added new features to the programming language for C. This had a library-like generic macro type, enhanced Unicode support, anonymous structures, multi-threading, bounds-checked functions and atomic structures. It had improved compatibility with C++. Some parts of the C99 library in C11 were made optional.

The Embedded C programming language included a few features that were not part of C. These included the named address spaces, basic I/O hardware addressing and fixed point arithmetic.

C Programming Language Features

There are a lot of features of the programming language, which include the following:

- Modularity

- Interactivity

- Portability

- Reliability

- Effectiveness

- Efficiency

- Flexibility

Uses of the C Programming Language

This language has found several applications. It is now used for the development of system applications, which form a huge portion of operating systems such as Linux, Windows and UNIX.

Some of the applications of C language include the following:

- Spreadsheets

- Database systems

- Word processors

- Graphics packages

- Network drivers

- Compilers and Assemblers

- Operating system development

- Interpreters

Chapter 3 Understanding C Program

The C program has several features and steps in order for an output or function is carried out.

Basic Commands (for writing basic C Program)

The basic syntax and commands used in writing a simple C program include the following:

#include <stdio.h>

This command is a preprocessor. <stdio.h> stands for standard input output header file. This is a file from the C library, which is included before the C program is compiled.

int main()

Execution of all C program begins with this main function.

{

This symbol is used to indicate the start of the main function.

}

This indicates the conclusion of the main function.

/* */

Anything written in between this command will not be considered for execution and compilation.

printf (output);

The printf command prints the output on the screen.

getch();

Writing this command would allow the system to wait for any keyboard character input.

return 0

Writing this command will terminate the C program or main function and return to 0.

A basic C Program would look like this:

```
#include <stdio.h>
int main()
{
/* Our first simple C basic program */
printf("Hello People! ");
getch();
return 0;
}
```

The output of this simple program would look like this:

Hello People!

Chapter 4 Learn C Programming

After learning the basic elements and what the language is all about, time to start programming in C. Here are the most important steps:

Download a compiler

A compiler is a program needed to compile the C code. It interprets the written codes and translates it into specific signals, which can be understood by the computer. Usually, compiler programs are free. There are different compilers available for several operating systems. Microsoft Visual Studio and MinGW are compilers available for Windows operating systems. XCode is among the best compilers for Mac. Among the most widely used C compiler options for Linux is gcc.

Basic Codes

Consider the following example of a simple C program in the previous chapter:

```
#include <stdio.h>


int main()

{

    printf("Hello People!\n");

    getchar();

    return o;

}
```

At the start of the program, #include command is placed. This is important in order to load the libraries where the needed functions are located.

The <stdio.h> refers to the file library and allows for the use of the succeeding functions getchar() and printf().

21

The command int main () sends a message to the compiler to run the function with the name "main" and return a certain integer once it is done running. Every C program executes a main function.

The symbol { } is used to specify that everything within it is a component of the "main" function that the compiler should run.

The function printf() tells the system to display the words or characters within the parenthesis onto the computer screen. The quotation marks make certain that the C compiler would print the words or characters as it is. The sequence \n informs the C compiler to place its cursor to the succeeding line. At the conclusion of the line, a ; (semicolon) is placed to denote that the sequence is done. Most codes in C program needs a semicolon to denote where the line ends.

The command getchar() informs the compiler to stop once it reaches the end of the function and standby for an input from the keyboard before continuing. This command is very useful because most compilers would run the C program and then immediately exits the window. The getchar() command would prevent the compiler to close the window until after a keystroke .is made.

The command return o denotes that the function has ended. For this particular C program, it started as an int, which indicates that the program has to return an integer once it is done running. The "o" is an indication that the compiler ran the program correctly. If another number is returned at the end of the program, it means that there was an error somewhere in the program.

Compiling the program

To compile the program, type the code into the program's code editor. Save this as a type of *.c file, then click the Run or Build button.

Commenting on the code

Any comments placed on codes are not compiled. These allow the user to give details on what happens in the function. Comments are good reminders on what the code is all about and for what. Comments also help other developers to understand what the code when they look at it.

To make a comment, add a /* at the beginning of the comment. End the written comment with a */. When commenting, comment on everything except the basic portions of the code, where explanations are no longer necessary because the meanings are already clearly understood.

Also, comments can be utilized for quick removal of code parts without having to delete them. Just enclose portions of the code in /* */, then compile. Remove these tags if these portions are to be added back into the code.

USING VARIABLES

Understanding variables

Define the variables before using them. Some common ones include char, float and int.

Declaring variables

Again, variables have to be declared before the program can use them. To declare, enter data type and then the name of the variable. Take a look at these examples:

```
char name;

float x;

int f, g, i, j;
```

Multiple variables can also be declared all on a single line, on condition that all of them belong to the same data type. Just separate the names of the variables commas (i.e., int f, g, i, j;).

When declaring variables, always end the line with a semicolon to denote that the line has ended.

Location on declaring the variables

Declaring variables is done at the start of the code block. This is the portion of the code enclosed by the brackets {}. The program won't function well if variables are declared later within the code block.

Variables for storing user input

Simple programs can be written using variables. These programs will store inputs of the user. Simple programs will use the function scanf, which searches the user's input for particular values. Take a look at this example:

```c
#include <stdio.h>


int main()

{

int x;


printf( "45: " );

scanf( "%d", &x );

printf( "45 %d", x );

getchar();

return 0;

}
```

The string &d informs the function scanf to search the input for any integers.

The command & placed before the x variable informs the function scanf where it can search for the specific variable so that the function can change it. It also informs the function to store the defined integer within the variable.

The last printf tells the compiler to read back the integer input into the screen as a feedback for the user to check.

Manipulating variables

Mathematical expressions can be used, which allow users to manipulate stored variables. When using mathematical expressions, it is most important to remember to use the "=" distinction. A single = will set the variable's value. A == (double equal sign) is placed when the goal is to compare the values on both sides of the sign, to check if the values are equal.

For example:

x = 2 * 4; /* sets the value of "x" to 2 * 4, or 8 */

x = x + 8; /* adds 8 to the original "x " value, and defines the new "x" value as the specific variable */

x == 18; /* determines if the value of "x" is equal to 18 */

x < 11; /* determines if the "x" value is lower than 11 */

CONDITIONAL STATEMENTS

Conditional statements can also be used within the C program. In fact, most programs are driven by these statements. These are determined as either False or True and then acted upon depending on the results. The most widely used and basic conditional statement is if.

In C, False and True statements are treated differently. Statements that are "TRUE" are those that end up equal to nonzero numbers. For example, when a comparison is performed, the outcome is a "TRUE" statement if the returned numerical value is "1". The result is a "FALSE" statement if the value that returns is "0".

Basic conditional operators

The operation of conditional statements is based on mathematical operators used in comparing values. The most common conditional operators include the following:

< /* less than */

6 < 15 TRUE

> /* greater than */

10 > 5 TRUE

<= /* less than or equal to */

4 <= 8 TRUE

>= /* greater than or equal to */

8 >= 8 TRUE

!= /* not equal to */

4 != 5 TRUE

== /* equal to */

7 == 7 TRUE

How to write a basic "IF" conditional statement

A conditional "IF" statement is used in determining what the next step in the program is after evaluation of the statement. These can be combined with other types of conditional statements in order to create multiple and powerful options.

Take a look at this example:

```
#include <stdio.h>


int main()

{

 if ( 4 < 7 )

   printf( "4 is less than 7");

   getchar();

}
```

The "ELSE/ELSE IF" statements

These statements can be used in expanding the conditional statements. Build upon the "IF" statements with "ELSE" and "ELSE IF" type of conditional statements, which will handle different types of results. An "ELSE" statement will be run when the IF statement result is FALSE. An "ELSE IF" statement will allow for the inclusion of multiple IF statements in one code block, which will handle all the various cases of the statement.

Take a look at this example:

```c
#include <stdio.h>

int main()
{
  int age;

  printf( "Please type current age: " );
  scanf( "%d", &age );
  if ( age <= 10 ) {
    printf( "You are just a kid!\n" );
  }
  else if ( age < 30 ) {
    printf( "Being a young adult is pretty awesome!\n" );
  }
  else if ( age < 50 ) {
    printf( "You are young at heart!\n" );
  }
  else {
    printf( "Age comes with wisdom.\n" );
  }
  return 0;
```

```
}
```

The above program will take all the input from the user and will run it through the different defined IF statements. If the input (number) satisfies the 1st IF statement, the 1st printf statement will be returned. If it does not, then input will be run through each of the "ELSE IF" statements until a match is found. If after all the "ELSE IF" statements have been run and nothing works, the input will be run through the "ELSE" statement at the last part of the program.

LOOPS

Loops are among the most important parts of C programming. These allow the user to repeat code blocks until particular conditions have been met. Loops make implementing repeated actions easy and reduce the need to write new conditional statements each time.

There are 3 main types of loops in C programming. These are FOR, WHILE and Do... WHILE.

"FOR" Loop

The "FOR" loop is the most useful and commonly used type of loop in C programming. This loop continues to run the function until the conditions set for this loop are met. There are 3 conditions required by the FOR loop. These include initialization of the variable, meeting the condition and how updating of the variable is done. All of these conditions need not be met at the same time, but a blank space with semicolon is still needed to prevent the loop from running continuously.

Take a look at this example:

```c
#include <stdio.h>


int main()

{

int y;


for ( y = 0; y < 10; y++;){
```

```c
    printf( "%d\n", y );

}

getchar();

}
```

The value of y has been set to 0, and the loop is programmed to continue running as long as the y value remains less than 10. At each run (loop), the y value is increased by 1 before the loop is repeated. Hence, once the value of y is equivalent to 10 (after 10 loops), the above loop will then break.

WHILE Loop

These are simpler than the FOR loops. There is only one condition, which is that as long as the condition remains TRUE, the loop continues to run. Variables need not to be initialized or updated, but can be done within the loop's main body.

Take a look at this example:

```c
#include <stdio.h>


int main()

{

int y;


while ( y <= 20 ){

printf( "%d\n", y );

y++;

}
```

```
getchar();

}
```

In the above program, the command y++ will add 1 to the variable *y* for each execution of the loop. When the value of *y* reaches 21, the loop will break.

DO...WHILE Loop

This is a very useful loop to ensure at least 1 run. FOR and WHILE loops check the conditions at the start of the loop, which ensures that it could not immediately pass and fail. DO...WHILE loops will check the conditions when the loop is finished. This ensures that the loop will run at last once before a pass and fail occurs.

Take a look at this example:

```
#include <stdio.h>


int main()

{

int y;


y = 10;

do {

  printf("This loop is running!\n");

} while ( y != 10 );

getchar();

}
```

This type of loop displays the message whether the condition results turn out TRUE or FALSE. The *y* variable is set to 10. The WHILE loop has been set to run when the y value is not equal to 10, at which the loop ends. The message was printed because the condition is not checked until the loop has ended.

The WHILE portion of the DO..WHILE loop must end with a semicolon. This is also the only instance when a loop ends this way.

Conclusion

Thank you again for purchasing this book!

I hope this book was able to help you to understand the complex terms and language used in C. this programming method can put off a lot of users because of its seemingly complexity. However, with the right basic knowledge, soon, you will be programming more complex things with C.

The next step is to start executing these examples. Reading and understanding this book is not enough, although this will push you into the right direction. Execution will cement the knowledge and give you the skill and deeper understanding of C.

Finally, if you enjoyed this book, please take the time to share your thoughts and post a review on Amazon. We do our best to reach out to readers and provide the best value we can. Your positive review will help us achieve that. It'd be greatly appreciated!

Thank you and good luck!

Book 2
Rails Programming
Professional Made Easy

BY SAM KEY

Expert Rails Programming Success In A Day For Any Computer User!

Programming Box Set #25: C Programming Professional Made Easy & Rails Programming Professional Made Easy

Table Of Contents

Introduction... 36

Chapter 1 Why Rails Matters 37

Chapter 2 Getting Started 39

Chapter 3 Create Your First Project....................................41

Chapter 4 Say "Hello There!" 44

Chapter 5 Let's Do Something More................................... 46

Chapter 6 Creating Article Title 47

Chapter 7 Creating the Form 48

Chapter 8 Save Your Data..51

Chapter 9 Make Your Articles Neat....................................53

Chapter 10 Create Some Rules, Too 55

Chapter 11 Update Articles..57

Chapter 12 Destroy Some Data.. 60

Conclusion 63

Check out My Other Books.. 64

Introduction

I want to thank you and congratulate you for purchasing the book, "insert book title here Professional Rails Programming Made Easy: Expert Rails Programming Success In A Day For Any Computer User!"

This book contains proven steps and strategies on how to learn the program Ruby on Rails and immediately create an application by applying the rudiments of this platform.

Rails is one of the newest and most popular platforms. Thanks to the growth of Internet, this platform has been targeting audiences that are quite interested in creating stable web designs. If your work involves the Internet and you want to implement ideas that would help you launch projects online, you would definitely want to learn how to code using this program. Within this book are everything that you need to learn from installing the platform, getting the basics and making sure that you are ready to rock any programmer's boat.

Thanks again for purchasing this book. I hope you enjoy it!

Chapter 1 Why Rails Matters

If you are a computer programmer, the Ruby on Rails platform would probably the next program that you have to learn how to use. It is also worth looking into if your work is largely based on design, and you want to try something current to make websites easy to manipulate and beautiful. It could also be the platform that would launch your career or create leverage for yourself at the office. Yes, this platform could be your trump card to your next promotion, or that awesome site that you have in mind.

What Rails Can Do For You

If you are wondering what good this program can do for most computer users, then here are the awesome things that you can get out of the platform.

1. Get to Code

Coding is not rocket science, and if you are using Ruby, you probably would not even feel that you are using a programming language. You would want to learn to code to retain what you are going to experience with the platform, so take the time to study anyway.

If you are getting into Rails, you do not need to be a Computer Science major. If you are a businessman who has a great idea for a web app and you want to try coding it yourself, then this platform may be your best bet.

2. Get to Code Better

Sometimes it is not about arguing what is the best platform out there and get drunk arguing which is the best among Python, Java, PHP, or Ruby. If you already know other programming languages, you would need to still keep up with the times and learn some new tricks. Ruby on Rails provides that opportunity.

3. Get to Code Faster

RoR is a beautiful platform that allows you to write shorter codes, and it has a great set of features for exception handling which makes it really easy to spot and handle possible errors. You also would not need to still maintain the usual reference counts in your extension libraries. You also get awesome support using Ruby from C, which gives you better handle when you want to write C extensions.

RoR makes any programmer productive because it is opinionated and it gives guesses on how you can probably code something in the best way possible. The Don't Repeat Yourself (DRY) Principle of RoR also makes you skip the usual coding process of writing something again and again, which often makes the code long, complex, and difficult to debug. That means that at the end of the project, you get to look at your code and have a better grasp of what happened there.

4. Understand How Twitter Works

Yes, Twitter is created using RoR, and if you are an SEO specialist, a web designer, or simply a tech geek, knowing how this social media platform is done would definitely help you out. You would also discover that a lot of the hot new websites today are built on this platform.

5. Learn a Platform with a Great Community

RoR is relatively young compared to other programming languages, and for that reason, it has a very active and collaborative community. You definitely would get to hang out with several other developers and would probably build something together. Doing that is always good for your résumé.

6. It works with all operating systems and offers threading that is independent from the operating system. That means that is also very portable, and would even work on a computer that runs on Windows 95.

If these perks sound great, then it's time to get started with a Rails project!

Chapter 2 Getting Started

If you want to learn how to use Rails, then you would need to first have the following:

1. Ruby – choose the language version that is 1.9.3, or later. You can download it by visiting ruby-lang.org.

2. RubyGems packaging system – it is typically installed with Ruby that has versions 1.9 or newer.

3. Installed SQLite3 Database

Rails, as you probably figured out, is a framework dedicated to web application development written in the language of Ruby. That means that you would want to learn a little bit of Ruby coding in order to eliminate any difficulty in jumping into Rails. If you have a browser open, you can get great help in practicing Ruby codes by logging in to tryruby.org, which features a great interactive web tutorial. Try it out first to get the hang out of coding with Ruby.

If you do not have any working SQLite 3 yet, you can find it at sqlite.org. You can also get installation instructions there.

Installing Rails

1. Run the Rails installer (for Windows and Mac users) or the Tokaido (Mac OS X users)

2. Check out the version of the installed Ruby on your computer by running the Run command on Start menu and then typing cmd on the prompt (Windows). If you are running on Mac OS X, launch Terminal.app.

Key in "$ ruby –v" (no captions). After you hit Enter, you will see the Ruby version installed

3. Check out the version of SQLite3 installed by typing "$ sqlite3 –version".

4. After Rails installation, type in "$ rails –version" on Terminal.app or at the command prompt. If it says something similar to Rails 4.2.0, then you are good to go.

A Note on the $ sign

The $ sign would be used here in this book to look like the terminal prompt where you would type your code after. If you are using Windows for the Rails platform, you would see something like this: c:\source_code> .

Chapter 3 Create Your First Project

Here's something that most web developers are raving about Rails: it comes with generators, or scripts that are made to make development a lot easier by making all things that you need to get started on a particular project. Among these scripts is the new application generator, which gives you the foundation you need for a new Rails app so you do not have to write one yourself. Now that allows you to jump right into your code!

Since you are most likely to build a website or an API (application program interface), you would want to start coding a blog application. To start, launch a terminal and go to any directory where you can create files. On the prompt, type "$ rails new blog."

After you hit Enter, Rails will start making an application called Blog in the directory. It will also start making gem dependencies that you already have in your Gemfile bundle install.

Now, go to where your blog app is by typing in "$ cd blog".

What's in There?

Once you get into the directory, you will find a number of files that Rails have already installed by default. If you are not quite sure about what these files are for, here's a quick rundown of the file or folder functions:

1. app/ - this has the models, helpers, mailers, assets, and controllers for the app you just created. You'll be looking more at this folder later.

2. bin/ - this has the script that you will use to run the app. Also, this has other scripts that you will be using to deploy, setup, or run the application you are going to create.

3. config/ - this allows you to tweak the app's database, routes, etc.

4. config.ru – this is the configuration that will be used by Rack-based servers to run the app.

5. db/ - this would contain your database and database migrations

6. Gemfile, Gemfile.lock – these would allow you to tell the program what sort of gem dependencies you are going to need for the app you're building.

7. lib/ - contains the extended modules needed for the app

8. lib – contains the app's log files

9. public/ – this would be the sole folder that other people could see. It would be containing all your compiled assets and created static files.

10. Rakefile – this would be the one file that would locate and load tasks that can be set to run from the command line. You can add tasks that you would prefer to use later on by adding the files needed to the lib/tasks directory

11. README.rdoc – just like readme's function, this would be a brief document that would tell other people how your app works, how to set it up, etc.

12. test/ - these would contain all your unit tests and all the things that you are going to need for testing.

13. tmp/ - this would hold all temporary files

14. vendor/ - this would contain all your third-party codes and would also contain all vendored gems.

Now, if you are seeing all these in the app directory you just made, then you are ready to create little bits and pieces that you would be adding up later to make a real blog app!

Firing Up the Web Server

Since you already have the barebones of your blog application, you would want to set up how the app is going to be launched on the internet. To start a web server go to the directory where blog is located, and then type "$ bin/rails server".

Important note:

You would need to have a JavaScript runtime available in your computer if you want to use asset compression for JavaScript or if you want to compile a CoffeeScript. Otherwise, you would expect to see an execjs error when you attempt to compile these assets. If you want to look at all the supported runtimes, you can go to github.com/sstephenson/execjs#readme.

If you are successful, what you just did would launch WEBrick, which is the server that Ruby apps use by default. You can see what's happening so far in your app by firing up a web browser and typing http://localhost:3000. Now, since you have done nothing much, you would be seeing the Rails default page. It will tell you that you are currently in development mode. You also do not need to constantly require the server to look at the changes that you have made – any changes will be automatically picked up and seen. Also keep in mind that if you managed to see this "Welcome Aboard" thing, you are sure that you created an app that is configured correctly. If you want to find out the app's environment, click on "About your application's environment" link.

Got everything right so far? Let's move on to making something other people can read.

Chapter 4 Say "Hello There!"

If you want to make Rails learn how to say Hi to other people, you would need the following:

1. A controller

The purpose of a controller is to allow your program to receive any requests. When you route, you enable Rails to decide which of the controllers you set up will receive which types of requests. That may also mean that there would be different routes leading to the controller, which would be triggered by specific actions. An action is required in order to collect any information needed in order to send it to a view

2. A view

This thing's main purpose is to enable Rails to display the information made available to the action and display it in a format that other people can read. There are different view templates that are already available and coded using eRuby, which can be used in request cycles before it the information is sent to anyone who wants to look at this information.

Got it? Good. Now, to setup your welcome page, you need to generate a controller and then name it "welcome" using an action named "index". Your code will look like this:

$ bin/rails generate controller welcome index

Now, Rails will be creating a bunch of files plus a route for you to use. When Rails is done with that, you will see this:

```
create  app/controllers/welcome_controller.rb
 route  get 'welcome/index'
invoke  erb
create    app/views/welcome
create    app/views/welcome/index.html.erb
invoke  test_unit
create    test/controllers/welcome_controller_test.rb
invoke  helper
create    app/helpers/welcome_helper.rb
invoke  assets
invoke    coffee
create      app/assets/javascripts/welcome.js.coffee
```

```
invoke  scss
create  app/assets/stylesheets/welcome.css.scss
```

If you want to view where the course of your controller is, go to app/controllers/welcome_controller.rb. If you want to look at the view, you can find it at app/views/welcome/index.html.erb.

Here comes the fun part. Pull up a text editor and open app/views/welcome/index.html.erb there. Clear all the codes you see there, and replace it with this:

```
<h1>Hello Rails!</h1>
```

After doing so, you have successfully informed Rails that you want "Hello Rails!" to appear. That means that it is also the greeting that you want to see when you go to http://localhost:3000, which is still displaying "Welcome aboard".

Create the App's Home Page

The next thing that you need to do is to tell Rails where the home page is. To do that, pull up your text editor again and open config/routes.rb. You should see something like this:

```
Rails.application.routes.draw do
get 'welcome/index'

# The priority is based upon order of creation:
# first created -> highest priority.
#
# You can have the root of your site routed with "root"
# root 'welcome#index'
#
# ...
```

Those lines represent the routing file which tells Rails how to link requests to specific actions and controllers. Now, find the line "root 'welcome#index'" and uncomment it. When you get back to http://localhost:3000, you will see that it now displays Hello Rails!

Chapter 5 Let's Do Something More

Now that you have figured out how to make a controller, a view, and an action, it's time to create a new resource. A resource is something that groups together similar objects the same way you group people, plants, and animals. To make items for resources, you use the CRUD method (create, read, update, destroy).

Rails make it easy for you to build websites because it already comes with a method for resources that it can use for making a REST resource. REST, or Representational State Transfer is known as the web's architectural structure which is used to design all applications that use a network, and instead of using rather complex operations to link two machines, you can use HTTP to make machines communicate. That means that in a lot of ways, the Internet is based on a RESTful design.

Now, following the project you are creating, pull up config/routes.rb and make sure it's going to look like this:

> **Rails.application.routes.draw do**
>
> **resources :articles**
>
> **root 'welcome#index'**
> **end**

If you are going to look at the rake routes, you will notice that Rails has already made routes for all actions involving REST. It is going to look like this:

```
$ bin/rake routes
      Prefix Verb   URI Pattern              Controller#Action
     articles GET   /articles(.:format)          articles#index
          POST /articles(.:format)        articles#create
  new_article GET   /articles/new(.:format)      articles#new
 edit_article GET   /articles/:id/edit(.:format) articles#edit
      article GET   /articles/:id(.:format)      articles#show
          PATCH /articles/:id(.:format)     articles#update
          PUT   /articles/:id(.:format)     articles#update
          DELETE /articles/:id(.:format)     articles#destroy
         root GET   /                        welcome#index
```

Chaper 6 Creating Article Title

This part would be the creating and reading part of CRUD, where you would put in a location where you would be placing articles for the blog you're building. In order to do so, you can create an ArticlesController by running this code:

$ bin/rails g controller articles

Now, you need to manually place an action inside the controller that you just created. Go to app/controllers/articles_controller.rb and pull up the class ArticlesController. Edit it to look like this:

```
class ArticlesController < ApplicationController

 def new

 end

end
```

You now have to create a template that Rails would be able to view. In order to create a title for the article that you want to display, pull up app/views/articles/new.html.erb and make a new file there. Type the following:

```
<h1>New Article</h1>
```

What did just happen? Check out http://localhost:3000/articles/new and you will see that the page now has a title! You will now want to create a template that will look like a form that you can fill up to write your articles in online.

Chapter 7 Creating the Form

Pull up app/views/articles/new.html.erb and then add this code:

```
<%= form_for :article do |f| %>
<p>
 <%= f.label :title %><br>
 <%= f.text_field :title %>
</p>

<p>
 <%= f.label :text %><br>
 <%= f.text_area :text %>
</p>

<p>
 <%= f.submit %>
</p>
<% end %>
```

You will see that you have just created a form that has a space for the article title text, submit button, and it comes with boxes too! That is the function of the code form_for. You will realize that when you submit an article you are going to create, it needs to be done in another URL and then the entire text should then go somewhere else. Edit app/views/articles/new.html.erb by finding the form_for line and make it look like this:

```
<%= form_for :article, url: articles_path do |f| %>
```

In Rails, the action "create" does the job of making new forms for submissions, and therefore, your form should be working towards this action. You would notice that when you try to submit an article, you would see an error there. In order to make it work, you need to make a "create action" within the ArticlesController.

Create the Article

In order to get rid of this error, you need to edit the ArticlesController class found in app/controllers/articles_controller.rb. It should look like this:

```
class ArticlesController < ApplicationController
   def new
```

```
        end

        def create
        end
    end
```

Once that is done, the controller should now be able to save the article to the database. Now, you would need to set the parameters of actions done by controllers. Now, make the ending of the above lines to look like this instead:

```
        def create
          render plain: params[:article].inspect
        end
```

Now that should make the error go away. Try refreshing the page to see what happened.

Make the Model

Rails already provide a generator that would be used by your project to launch a model. To order Rails to start generating one, run this on the terminal:

```
$ bin/rails generate model Article title:string text:text
```

What just happened is that you told Rails that you are requiring an Article model that has a title and a text that are attributed to separate strings. You would see that the platform made up a lot of files, but you would be most interested in db/migrate/20140120191729_create_articles.rb which contains your blog's database.

Now, you would want to run a migration, which you can do with a single line of code:

```
$ bin/rake db:migrate
```

What Rails would do is that it would be executing this command which means that it made the Articles Table:

```
==                           CreateArticles:           migrating
================================================
====
-- create_table(:articles)
```

```
  -> 0.0019s
== 		CreateArticles: 	migrated 	(0.0020s)
==========================================
```

Chapter 8 Save Your Data

Pull up app/controllers/articles_controller.rb and edit the "create" action into this:

```
def create
 @article = Article.new(params[:article])

 @article.save
 redirect_to @article
end
```

You're almost able to create an article! However, when you refresh the page, you would see a Forbidden Attributes Error, and would point you at the line @article – Article.new(params[:article]). The reason Rails is giving you a hard time is because it wants you to tell what parameters should be in your controller actions. That allows your program to be secure once you run it, and prevent it from assigning wrong controller parameters which can make your entire coded program crash.

To fix this, edit out the highlighted line in the error you just saw and change it into:

```
@article = Article.new(params.require(:article).permit(:title, :text))
```

Show Your Work

In order to make the page display your article, you can make use of the "show" action by adding it to app/controllers/articles_controller.rb. Add these following lines:

```
class ArticlesController < ApplicationController
 def show
  @article = Article.find(params[:id])
 end

 def new
 end
```

Now let's add some style. Create a new file named app/views/articles/show.html.erb and put in the following lines:

```
<p>
 <strong>Title:</strong>
 <%= @article.title %>
</p>

<p>
 <strong>Text:</strong>
 <%= @article.text %>
</p>
```

Refresh http://localhost:3000/articles/new and then you will see that you can create articles and display them!

Chapter 9 Make Your Articles Neat

Find a way to list all the articles that you are going to create in order to have an organized database. To do that, pull up app/controllers/articles_controller.rb and add the following lines to create a control.

```
class ArticlesController < ApplicationController
  def index
    @articles = Article.all
  end

  def show
    @article = Article.find(params[:id])
  end

  def new
  end
```

Now, to add a view, pull up app/views/articles/index.html.erb and then add the following lines:

```
<h1>Article List</h1>

<table>
  <tr>
    <th>Title</th>
    <th>Text</th>
  </tr>

  <% @articles.each do |article| %>
    <tr>
      <td><%= article.title %></td>
      <td><%= article.text %></td>
    </tr>
  <% end %>
</table>
```

Head over to http://localhost:3000/articles and you will see all the articles that you have made so far.

Tidy Up Some More with Links

You definitely need to create links for the articles that you have created so your readers can pull them up easily. To add links, open app/views/welcome/index.html.erb and then change it to look like this:

```
<h1>Hello, Rails!</h1>
<%= link_to 'My Blog', controller: 'articles' %>
```

Now, what if you want to add a link that would allow you to write a new article right away? All you need to do is to add the following lines to app/views/articles/index.html.erb to have a New Article link:

```
%= link_to 'New article', new_article_path %>
```

If you want to create a link to go back to where you were previously, add the following lines to the same file:

```
<%= form_for :article, url: articles_path do |f| %>
...
<% end %>

<%= link_to 'Back', articles_path %>
```

Chapter 10 Create Some Rules, Too

When you are creating a blog program, you do not want your users to accidentally submit a blank page, and then just land right back where they were without knowing what they did. Rails can help you make sure that doesn't happen by editing the app/models/article.rb file to look like this:

```
class Article < ActiveRecord::Base
  validates :title, presence: true,
              length: { minimum: 5 }
end
```

That means that the title should be at least 5 characters in order for the article to go through, otherwise it would not be saved. Now that this rule for your blog is in place, you need to show the blog user that something went wrong and that the form should be filled up properly. To do that, tweak the "create" and "new" actions in app/controllers/articles_controller.rb in order to look like this:

```
def new
  @article = Article.new
end

def create
  @article = Article.new(article_params)

  if @article.save
    redirect_to @article
  else
    render 'new'
  end
end

private
  def article_params
    params.require(:article).permit(:title, :text)
  end
```

What just happened is that you told Rails that if the user did not type in 5 characters in the Title field, it should show the blank form again to the user. That doesn't offer much help. In order to tell the user what went wrong, edit the app/controllers/articles_controller.rb file again and to cater the following changes:

```
def create
```

```ruby
  @article = Article.new(article_params)

  if @article.save
    redirect_to @article
  else
    render 'new'
  end
end

def update
  @article = Article.find(params[:id])

  if @article.update(article_params)
    redirect_to @article
  else
    render 'edit'
  end
end

private
  def article_params
    params.require(:article).permit(:title, :text)
  end
```

Now, to show this to the user, tweak the app/views/articles/index.html.erb file and add the following lines:

```erb
<table>
  <tr>
    <th>Title</th>
    <th>Text</th>
    <th colspan="2"></th>
  </tr>

  <% @articles.each do |article| %>
    <tr>
      <td><%= article.title %></td>
      <td><%= article.text %></td>
      <td><%= link_to 'Show', article_path(article) %></td>
      <td><%= link_to 'Edit', edit_article_path(article) %></td>
    </tr>
  <% end %>
</table>
```

Chapter 11 Update Articles

You would expect your users to change their minds about the article that they just wrote and make some changes. This would involve the Update action in CRUD, which would prompt you to add an edit action in the ArticlesController and add this function between the "create" and "new" actions. It should look like this:

```ruby
def new
 @article = Article.new
end

def edit
 @article = Article.find(params[:id])
end

def create
 @article = Article.new(article_params)

 if @article.save
  redirect_to @article
 else
  render 'new'
 end
end
```

To allow a view for this, create a file and name it app/views/articles/edit.html.erb and then put in the following lines:

```erb
<h1>Editing article</h1>

<%= form_for :article, url: article_path(@article), method: :patch do |f| %>

 <% if @article.errors.any? %>
  <div id="error_explanation">
   <h2>
    <%= pluralize(@article.errors.count, "error") %> prohibited
    this article from being saved:
   </h2>
   <ul>
    <% @article.errors.full_messages.each do |msg| %>
     <li><%= msg %></li>
    <% end %>
```

```
  </ul>
  </div>
<% end %>

<p>
  <%= f.label :title %><br>
  <%= f.text_field :title %>
</p>

<p>
  <%= f.label :text %><br>
  <%= f.text_area :text %>
</p>

<p>
  <%= f.submit %>
</p>

<% end %>

<%= link_to 'Back', articles_path %>
```

Now, you would need to create the "update" action in app/controllers/articles_controller.rb. Edit the file to look like this:

```
def create
  @article = Article.new(article_params)

  if @article.save
    redirect_to @article
  else
    render 'new'
  end
end

def update
  @article = Article.find(params[:id])

  if @article.update(article_params)
    redirect_to @article
  else
    render 'edit'
  end
end

private
```

```ruby
def article_params
  params.require(:article).permit(:title, :text)
end
```

In order to show a link for Edit, you can edit app/views/articles/index.html.erb to make the link appear after the Show link.

```erb
<table>
 <tr>
  <th>Title</th>
  <th>Text</th>
  <th colspan="2"></th>
 </tr>

 <% @articles.each do |article| %>
  <tr>
   <td><%= article.title %></td>
   <td><%= article.text %></td>
   <td><%= link_to 'Show', article_path(article) %></td>
   <td><%= link_to 'Edit', edit_article_path(article) %></td>
  </tr>
 <% end %>
</table>
```

Now, to give chance for the user to Edit his work, add these lines to the template app/views/articles/show.html.erb:

...

```erb
<%= link_to 'Back', articles_path %> |
<%= link_to 'Edit', edit_article_path(@article) %>
```

Chapter 12 Destroy Some Data

No, it does not mean that you have to ruin the entire program you built. At this point, you would need to make provisions for the user to delete some of the articles that he wrote. Since you are creating a RESTful program, you would need to use the following route:

DELETE /articles/:id(.:format)   articles#destroy

This route makes it easy for Rails to destroy resources and you would need to make sure that it is placed before the protected or private methods. Let's add this action to the app/controllers/articles_controller.rb file:

```
def destroy
  @article = Article.find(params[:id])
  @article.destroy

  redirect_to articles_path
end
```

After doing so, you would notice that the ArticlesController in app/controllers/articles_controller.rb will now appear this way:

```
class ArticlesController < ApplicationController
  def index
    @articles = Article.all
  end

  def show
    @article = Article.find(params[:id])
  end

  def new
    @article = Article.new
  end

  def edit
    @article = Article.find(params[:id])
  end

  def create
```

```ruby
  @article = Article.new(article_params)

  if @article.save
    redirect_to @article
  else
    render 'new'
  end
end

def update
  @article = Article.find(params[:id])

  if @article.update(article_params)
    redirect_to @article
  else
    render 'edit'
  end
end

def destroy
  @article = Article.find(params[:id])
  @article.destroy

  redirect_to articles_path
end

private
  def article_params
    params.require(:article).permit(:title, :text)
  end
end
```

Now, it's time for you to let the user know that they have this option. Pull up the app/views/articles/index.html.erb file and add the following lines:

```erb
<h1>Listing Articles</h1>
<%= link_to 'New article', new_article_path %>
<table>
 <tr>
  <th>Title</th>
  <th>Text</th>
  <th colspan="3"></th>
 </tr>

 <% @articles.each do |article| %>
```

```
<tr>
  <td><%= article.title %></td>
  <td><%= article.text %></td>
  <td><%= link_to 'Show', article_path(article) %></td>
  <td><%= link_to 'Edit', edit_article_path(article) %></td>
  <td><%= link_to 'Delete', article_path(article),
      method: :delete,
      data: { confirm: 'Are you sure?' } %></td>
</tr>
<% end %>
</table>
```

You would notice that you also added up a feature to make the user confirm whether he really would want to delete the submitted article. Now, in order to make the confirmation box appear, you need to make sure that you have the file jquery_ujs in your machine.

Conclusion

Thank you again for purchasing this book!

I hope this book was able to help you to grasp the basics of Ruby on Rails and allow you to create a webpage based on the codes and processes discussed in this book.

The next step is to discover other applications of the platform and learn other Rails techniques that would improve your program design and integration.

Finally, if you enjoyed this book, please take the time to share your thoughts and post a review on Amazon. We do our best to reach out to readers and provide the best value we can. Your positive review will help us achieve that. It'd be greatly appreciated!

Thank you and good luck!

Check Out My Other Books

Below you'll find some of my other popular books that are popular on Amazon and Kindle as well. Simply click on the links below to check them out. Alternatively, you can visit my author page on Amazon to see other work done by me.

C Programming Success in a Day

Python Programming Success in a Day

PHP Programming Professional Made Easy

HTML Professional Programming Made Easy

CSS Programming Professional Made Easy

Windows 8 Tips for Beginners

C Programming Professional Made Easy

JavaScript Programming Made Easy

Programming Box Set #25: C Programming Professional Made Easy & Rails Programming Professional Made Easy

C ++ Programming Success in a Day

If the links do not work, for whatever reason, you can simply search for these titles on the Amazon website to find them.

www.ingramcontent.com/pod-product-compliance
Lightning Source LLC
Chambersburg PA
CBHW061034050326
40689CB00012B/2825